HOLY UNTO THE LORD

REDISCOVERING THE
JOY OF HOLINESS

LUKE LEFEVRE

Holy Unto The Lord
© 2022 by Luke LeFevre

All rights reserved; no part of this publication may be reproduced, stored in a retrieval system, or transmitted in any form or by any means–electronic, mechanical, photocopy, recording, or any other, except for brief quotations in printed reviews without prior permission of the publisher.

Unless otherwise indicated, all scripture quotations are taken from the New Living Translation.
Copyright © 1996, 2004, 2015 by Tyndal House Foundation.

Published by Consecrate Publishing

Requests for information should be addressed to:
Luke LeFevre
info@consecratemovement.com

ACKNOWLEDGMENTS

I want to thank my wife, Rebecca, for the hours you have spent helping me write and create this book. I couldn't have done it without you. I love you so much.

I would like to thank Katie Beiden, Danny Rangel, & Joel Evrist for reading my drafts and for your incredibly valuable feedback.

I would like to thank Anna Cosand for helping edit this book. Thank you so much for giving of your time and talent to help make this book possible.

Lastly, I would like to thank Jonathan Pokluda for your extremely generous endorsement. Your voice and leadership is a gift to this generation.

TABLE OF CONTENTS

The Joy of Holiness	1
The Holiness of God	13
Holy Unto The Lord	21
Costly Worship	28
Where Is the Power of God?	35
In the World but Not of It	42
A Consecrated Generation	50
References	57

1

THE JOY OF HOLINESS

Because we have these promises, dear friends, let us cleanse ourselves from everything that can defile our body or spirit. And let us work towards complete holiness because we fear God.

2 CORINTHIANS 7:1

I have told you these things so that you will be filled with my joy. Yes, your joy will overflow!

JOHN 15:11

The enemy has sold our generation a lie. We've been convinced that holiness is a straightjacket that leads to lifelessness. But the truth is that the pursuit of holiness is actually one of the greatest keys to true, life-giving joy.

This book was written from a place of love for you and the Church and from a desire for believers in our generation to experience all that God has for us.

So let's jump in.

A Conversation on Culture

One of the great dangers I see facing the Church today is our lack of conviction over consuming what the culture around us is producing. The most common places I see this playing out are in the music we listen to and the shows and movies we watch.

There's an increasing trend that I've noticed in the Church over the past several years of highlighting the *imago Dei*, or the image of God, in culture. The suggestion is that all people are created in the image of God, including secular artists; therefore, there are redeemable aspects of the art they create.

This line of reasoning continues that, because part of God's nature is to create, those made in His image–which includes every human being–are being like God when they create.

This logic then goes further by saying that, while we as Christians may not agree with the lyrics of their songs or the content of their films, we can still appreciate their art as something that image-bearers of God have created.

While there are some truthful aspects to this ideology–like the fact that all of us are created in God's image and that our ability to create is a gift from our Creator–it becomes dangerous when Christians use this reasoning to excuse their participation in sin.

Celebrating the Art?

There's an artist who's a great example for this discussion. He has sold 170 million records worldwide and has had ten number-one albums and nine number-one songs. He may end up being the most popular and successful artist of our generation. Musically speaking, he's a genius.

But, although he is a musical success, his songs are profane and sexually immoral. The cover of his latest album, *Certified Lover Boy*, is simply a picture of twelve pregnant women emojis–a not-so-subtle nod to the idea that sex is casual and "lover boys" just might end up with multiple babies–by multiple women. By now you can probably guess the artist I'm referring to is Drake.

When confronted about listening to his songs that celebrate sexual immorality and are full of profane lyrics, a common response from Christians is, "I don't listen to the lyrics. I just appreciate Drake's talent as an artist."

I hear these same types of things coming from Christians regarding either culturally popular or critically acclaimed movies that include similar content, even movies or shows that border on the pornographic or, at the very least, celebrate sexually immoral relationships and include profane humor. Whether it be *Game of Thrones* or something that seems much more harmless, we convince ourselves that we can ignore the content to praise the artistry.

HOLY UNTO THE LORD

A great biblical example that reveals the error of this mindset can be found in the book of Daniel. In Chapter 3, we find the story of Shadrach, Meshach, and Abed-Nego. It begins like this:

> *King Nebuchadnezzar made a gold statue ninety feet tall and nine feet wide and set it up on the plain of Dura in the province of Babylon. Then he sent messages to the high officers, officials, governors, advisers, treasurers, judges, magistrates, and all the provincial officials to come to the dedication of the statue he had set up. So all these officials came and stood before the statue King Nebuchadnezzar had set up. Then a herald shouted out, "People of all races and nations and languages, listen to the king's command! When you hear the sound of the horn, flute, zither, lyre, harp pipes, and other musical instruments, bow to the ground to worship King Nebuchadnezzar's gold statue. Anyone who refuses to obey will immediately be thrown into a blazing furnace.*

DANIEL 3:1-6

So when all the officials, which included Shadrach, Meshach, and Abed-Nego, are brought before the statue, the masses begin to bow before the idol in obedience to the king's command. But as the sea of people begins to fall to their knees, these three young men are left standing, refusing to bow.

THE JOY OF HOLINESS

This is essentially a death sentence for these three men. When word gets back to the king, he commands that they be thrown into the furnace. Still, they will not bow.

If you know the rest of the story, you know that God miraculously rescues them from the fire. Even though they're thrown in, they're completely unharmed.

Now, you might be thinking, "I don't see the connection between this passage of Scripture and Drake's music."

Let's connect the dots.

The gold statue that Nebuchadnezzar had commissioned was no normal statue. It was made at the request of one of the most powerful, rich, and cultured kings in world history.

I'd like to suggest that Nebuchadnezzar's statue was quite possibly the greatest piece of art that had ever been created. It was NINETY feet tall! And made of solid gold! The level of craftsmanship and artistry that would have gone into this idol's creation must have been breathtaking.

But here's what we don't see from Shadrach, Meshach, and Abed-Nego. They don't respond, "What an amazing representation of the talents humanity possesses as God's image bearers! King Nebuchadnezzar, we don't necessarily agree with the heart behind the creation of this idol, but we would love to congratulate the artist who made this for you! We won't bow to worship, but we'll bow in participation because of the good and redeemable characteristics of this idol."

No, to Shadrach, Meshach, and Abed-Nego, this was not a reason to celebrate mankind's gifts as the imago Dei, but rather it was a representation of the profaning and corrupting of the gifts and talents that humanity possesses as creations of God.

They respond with a conviction that this image and the king's command to bow profane the name of the one, true God. Not only do they not celebrate it, they refuse to participate in celebrating and praising it, even in the face of a death sentence.

When we consume songs, movies, and shows that celebrate the very things God commands against (and even hates), we're inadvertently participating in that celebration. What we consume communicates to the world what we celebrate.

Work Towards Complete Holiness

As you're reading this chapter, it's possible that arguments are coming to mind as to why this is wrong. I may be wrong, but after studying the scriptures, I've had a hard time finding a way around this.

The Apostle Paul writes in 2 Corinthians:

> *And what union can there be between God's temple and idols? For we are the temple of the living God. As God said, "I will live in them and walk among them. I will be their God and they will be my people. Therefore, come out from among unbelievers, and*

> *separate yourselves from them, says the Lord. Don't touch their filthy things, and I will welcome you. And I will be your Father, and you will be my sons and daughters, says the Lord Almighty."*
>
> 2 CORINTHIANS 6:16-18

Now I want us to especially focus in on this next verse: "Because we have these promises, dear friends, let us cleanse ourselves from everything that can defile our body or spirit. And let us work towards complete holiness because we fear God"- (2 Corinthians 7:1).

"Let us work towards complete holiness…" This means that our participation is required. There's effort that's needed. And we're to aim for *complete* holiness, not *partial* holiness. Our goal is *completely* holy lives.

Will we ever live lives that are completely without sin? No, I don't believe so. But we should be growing in holiness day by day by the empowering grace of God and the power of the Holy Spirit.

Living in the Culture Without Looking like the Culture

Philippians 4:8 says, "And now, dear brothers and sisters, one final thing. Fix your thoughts on what is true, and honorable, and right, and pure, and lovely, and admirable. Think about things that are excellent and worthy of praise."

The things we watch and listen to regularly become what we meditate on, either consciously or subconsciously.

The things we meditate on shape our thoughts.

And what shapes our thoughts will eventually manifest in our actions through compromises, even small ones.

This is why the Word commands us, "Don't copy the behavior and customs of this world, but let God transform you into a new person *by changing the way you think*. Then you will learn to know God's will for you, which is good and pleasing and perfect" (Romans 12:2, emphasis added).

A Change of Appetite

When I was in high school, my family packed up the car and took a road trip to visit some family. During that season, I had been intensely pursuing God. I had been diligent to seek Him and desired to grow closer to Him. I was so hungry just to be in His presence.

While we were driving, I put in some earbuds and started playing music on my iPod Touch. (Remember those?) I started playing an album by Coldplay, one of my favorite bands at the time. And as the music played, I remember looking out the car window as we drove, and, all of a sudden, something inside me felt "off."

I couldn't seem to place what it was, but I had this sinking feeling in my stomach that seemed to say, "I shouldn't be listening to this." It felt so strange because Coldplay is probably the cleanest secular band on the planet. There wasn't anything sinful about listening to their music, but the feeling kept nagging at me.

I took out my earbuds and continued looking out the window, asking the Holy Spirit what was causing this internal discomfort. The songs made me feel depressed and heavy. And it was at that moment I realized that nothing about the songs had changed, but rather my appetite had.

Around that same time, I had stopped drinking soda. I'm not exactly sure why I decided to stop, but I did. It could've had something to do with trying to be more healthy, but I honestly don't remember. It definitely wasn't because I didn't enjoy soda anymore. There was nothing better than Mexican food and a cold Coca-Cola. However, instead of ordering a soda with my meal, I would get water.

And then, several months after only drinking water, I tried drinking a Coke. But this time it tasted different. It tasted like a thick, sugary syrup, not like the refreshing drink I had remembered. I could only take a couple of sips before I felt the effect it was having on my body.

That's what those songs felt like, because for the months leading up to that car ride, I had only been listening to worship music. I just wanted to be in the presence of God. And when I turned on that Coldplay album, its "taste" had changed. It didn't satisfy anymore. It was like I'd been drinking pure water for months and had just tried to drink a Coke.

In the 90s, there was a trend that went around where everyone started burning their secular CDs. This isn't what I'm proposing. Although I think the heart behind the movement was good, I believe it leaned towards legalism.

While I'm not telling you to go out and burn all of your secular music, I am telling you that if you pursue nearness to Jesus with everything inside of you, your appetite is going to change. What satisfies you will change. And after drinking the pure water of God's Word and presence, you'll thirst for Him more and more.

The Joy of Holiness

In John 15, Jesus has just been exhorting His followers to keep His commandments. And then He makes a statement that gives us a glimpse into the great love behind all of His commands. He says, "I have told you these things so that you will be filled with my joy. Yes, your joy will overflow!" (John 15:11).

All of God's commands lead to life, not lifelessness. The result of keeping Jesus' commands is not a dry, bleak life, but rather a life that overflows with the joy that comes from His presence.

Second Corinthians 7:1, which we just read, begins with these words: "Because we have these promises…" What promises? God promises that He will dwell in our midst, and we will be His people *if* we'll cleanse ourselves from everything that defiles our bodies and spirits, working towards complete holiness out of reverence for God.

This is a mind-blowing promise! The incomprehensibly holy, powerful, majestic, righteous God of the universe wants to be close to us. This is one of the most precious promises that God has given us. He wants to dwell in our very midst.

We can never *produce* true holiness and righteousness before God by our works and personal piety. This was only accomplished for us by Jesus' death and resurrection. However, we are called to *pursue* the holiness Jesus has empowered us to walk in by His grace and the power of His Holy Spirit.

In the words of John Owen, "Be killing sin, or sin will be killing you."[1]

To many, the pursuit of holiness seems like legalism, which is when we place more faith in our rule following to earn salvation than in the sacrifice of Jesus. But the true heart behind pursuing holiness has nothing to do with legalism and everything to do with love for Jesus and wanting to live near to Him. Our working towards complete holiness isn't salvational–it's relational.

Psalm 16:11 says, "In your presence there is *fullness* of joy" (emphasis added). It's in God's presence that true joy, life, and contentment are found. And it's not just joy but the *fullness* of joy.

A burning desire for holiness comes not from legalism, but from having tasted the goodness and glory of nearness to God. When you experience the joy of living in the presence of God, you never want to do anything that could compromise that. And this is where our passion for holiness comes from as believers.

The Heart Behind Holiness

As someone who works in student and young adult ministry, I often hear questions like, "So where's the line? I know sleeping with my boyfriend or girlfriend is a sin, but what about making out? I know watching pornagraphy is a sin, but what about movies or shows with inappropriate jokes and language?"

But I believe these are the wrong questions.

I think the right question to ask is not, "Where's the line?" or "How far can I go without sinning?" Rather, we should ask, "How close to God can I get?" and "What does the Word of God say I need to rid from my life, or add to my life, that will get me closer to Him?"

This is the heart behind holiness.

2

THE HOLINESS OF GOD

It was in the year King Uzziah died that I saw the Lord. He was sitting on a lofty throne, and the train of his robe filled the Temple. Attending him were mighty seraphim, each having six wings. With two wings they covered their faces, with two they covered their feet, and with two they flew. They were calling out to each other, "Holy, holy, holy is the LORD of Heaven's Armies! The whole earth is filled with his glory!"

ISAIAH 6:1-3

If you grew up in the South like I did, you were probably used to hearing Christians described as "God-fearing." When you asked if someone was a believer, you might get the response, "Oh yes, he's a God-fearin' man." Translation: He's a Christian.

But what does it mean to fear God? The Bible has a lot to say about the concept, but many in our generation have held it at arm's length because they don't understand how God can be loving and good, yet feared.

Many seem to believe that fearing God is like fearing an abusive parent. I've known several people who grew up with an alcoholic mom or dad. They never knew how their parents would come home. Sometimes they were in a good mood; other times, they'd come home drunk and belligerent. These people lived in constant fear because they never knew what their parents' intentions would be towards them.

Let me assure you; that couldn't be farther from what fearing God is like.

God is not a Father with ever-changing moods. God is constant. He's steady. He doesn't just have love *for* you; He *is* love (1 John 4:8). And His intentions are always good towards us—even His discipline. His intentions are to prosper us and to work all things together for our good (Jeremiah 29:11; Romans 8:28). But the reality is that while God is good, He's also holy.

Psalm 25:14 says, "The Lord is a friend to those who fear Him." What a promise! I don't know about you, but I want to be the Lord's friend. I want to know His heart and be in close relationship with Him. But this is a promise that's reserved for those who fear Him.

The Glory of God

A few years ago, I watched a documentary on sailing. The film interviewed sailors who had crossed some of the deepest, most treacherous parts of the ocean. But they

THE HOLINESS OF GOD

hadn't traveled in massive cargo ships or cruise liners; they had sailed in small boats either alone or with a small team.

These sailors told stories of waves the size of office buildings, waves so large that they made the biggest waves we've seen from the shore look like ripples in a bathtub.

When they spoke, you could see a deep awe and respect for the ocean in their eyes. Retelling the stories of their adventures revealed a deep reverence in their souls for the power and might of the seas.

As I continued to watch, I had a realization that those who have seen the ocean–and I mean *really* seen the ocean–don't talk about it casually. There's a different level of fear and trembling in their voice, but also of love and wonder, than those of us who have never really left the shore.

One sailor said, "Never in my life have I experienced such beauty and such fear at the same time."

What struck me about these sailors was that, while they had such a healthy fear of the ocean's power, they also had a longing to be near it. They couldn't stay away. There was a glory they'd experienced in the ocean's fearsomeness.

This is what it's like to fear God.

A great example of this is in the book of Ezekiel. One day the prophet Ezekiel is taken into heaven and gets a glimpse of God. When his vision concludes, he's so stunned and amazed that he goes to a small town and sits "overwhelmed" for seven entire days (Ezekiel 3:15)!

After Ezekiel describes what he has seen, he says, "Such was the likeness of the appearance of the glory of God" (Ezekiel 1:28 NKJV).

Notice Ezekiel doesn't say that he saw God. Nor does he say that he saw the *glory* of God. He doesn't even say he saw the *appearance of the glory* of God! He says he saw the *likeness… of the appearance… of the glory…* of God. And just that small glimpse caused him to fall on his face and sit overwhelmed for a whole week.

In the same way that those who have really seen the ocean don't approach it casually, those who have *really* seen and known God approach Him with a deep awe and reverence. If we treat God like He's the mild waves on the shore, it's likely that we don't have a clear understanding of who He actually is.

Romans 1:20 says, "For since the creation of the world God's invisible qualities—his eternal power and divine nature—have been clearly seen, being understood from what has been made."

God's glory and power can be clearly seen in the things He's created. And if the ocean in all its might demands such awe and reverence, how much more the all-powerful God who spoke it into existence!

Holy, Holy, Holy

Scripture gives us a glimpse into heaven in Isaiah 6 and Revelation 4. In both accounts, we see mighty angels circling the throne of God. As they fly, these angels cover their faces to shield themselves from the sheer brilliance of God's glory.

And when these mighty angels get just the smallest glimpse of God from behind the wings that shield their faces, there's one word that erupts from the innermost part of their beings as a shout from their lips.

Holy.

They do not shout *loving*. Or *good*. Or even *righteous* or *merciful* or *just*.

The word that overflows from their mouths is *holy*: "Each of these living beings had six wings, and their wings were covered all over with eyes, inside and out. Day after day and night after night they keep on saying, 'Holy, holy, holy is the Lord God, the Almighty—the one who always was, who is, and who is still to come'" (Revelation 4:8).

The great preacher Charles Spurgeon once said, "In holiness God is more clearly seen than in anything else, save in the Person of Christ Jesus the Lord, of whose life such holiness is but a repetition."[2]

So What Is Holiness?

For God to be holy means that He's separate. He's set apart. He's completely *other*. It means there's no one like Him. It means that He's unmatched in His transcendence. It means that He's the most righteous, most pure, most perfect, most good, most loving, and most just being in the universe. And there's no close second.

God's holiness and glory are like the brilliance and power of the sun. We're 93 million miles away from the sun, yet we can't even look at it without damaging our eyes. If we tried to get close to the sun, we would be incinerated while still millions upon millions of miles away.

In this way, the sun is set apart from us. The sun is made of something different than we are. Its very substance and makeup are, in a way, holy. Of course, I'm not saying the sun is holy in that it should be worshiped, but I *am* saying that it is different and more powerful than we are.

Perhaps one of the best descriptions of God's holiness that I've heard comes from C.S. Lewis' *The Lion, the Witch, and the Wardrobe*. In this book, God is represented by a lion named Aslan who helps to lead four siblings on a great journey. In this story there are talking animals, including a character named Mr. Beaver.

When the children are preparing to go meet Aslan for the first time, Susan, one of the siblings, becomes concerned as Mr. Beaver begins to describe him.

THE HOLINESS OF GOD

"Aslan is a lion–the Lion, the great Lion," Mr. Beaver says.

> Susan responds, "Ooh, I'd thought he was a man. Is he quite safe? I shall feel rather nervous about meeting a lion."
>
> "Safe?" says Mr. Beaver ... "Who said anything about safe? 'Course he isn't safe. But he's good."[3]

God is not safe. He's not a man. He's not like us. He's holy. But this is where we can find comfort: While He's not safe, He's good.

So What Does That Mean for Us?

Now, here's the real problem. God's holiness means that sin cannot exist in His presence. Sin can no more exist in God's presence than a gnat can fly to the heart of the sun. It's impossible.

In the Old Testament, when the high priest would go into the presence of God to offer sacrifices to the Lord, a rope would be tied around his ankle. The rope was there in case he had unconfessed sin in his life, causing him to drop dead in the holy presence of God. In such a scenario, the rope would be used to pull him out. Pretty intense.

And the problem goes deeper. God wants to be in a relationship of love and covenant with us, but we all have sin in our lives and have fallen short of God's holy, righteous standard (Romans 3:23).

HOLY UNTO THE LORD

So what does that mean for us? Firstly, it means that there's a great chasm that separates us from God and is impossible to cross because of our sinfulness and God's holiness... but thank God for Jesus!

It was Jesus' perfect, sinless, holy life and then His death on the cross that paid the penalty for the sins of all who would put their faith in Him and surrender their lives to Him as their Lord. Praise God for salvation through Jesus!

This means we can now draw near to God because of the righteousness that Jesus gave us through His death and resurrection. Hebrews 4:16 says, "So let us come boldly to the throne of our gracious God. There we will receive his mercy, and we will find grace to help us when we need it most."

Secondly–and it's important that we catch this–it means that just as God has always been holy, He is still holy. And that isn't something to be taken lightly. In Leviticus 10:3 the Word says, "This is what the Lord spoke, saying: 'By those who come near me I must be regarded as holy.'"

Those who draw near to God must not do so casually but with great awe and reverence.

It also means that, because God is holy, He empowers us by His Holy Spirit to live holy lives, free from the bondage and slavery of sin.

This is what we'll talk about in the chapters to come.

3

HOLY UNTO THE LORD

So get rid of all evil behavior. Be done with all deceit, hypocrisy, jealousy, and unkind speech. Like newborn babies, you must crave pure spiritual milk so that you will grow into a full experience of salvation... For you are a chosen people. You are royal priests, a holy nation, God's very own possession. As a result, you can show others the goodness of God, for he called you out of the darkness into his wonderful light.

1 PETER 2:1-2, 9

In the book of Exodus, God speaks to Moses and gives him specific instructions on how to prepare the people of Israel for something that would alter the course of human history—God was going to come and dwell in the midst of a group of people.

This had happened once before in the Garden of Eden. God had walked and talked with Adam and Eve until sin brought separation from the presence of God. Now, having just freed

HOLY UNTO THE LORD

the Israelites from slavery and bondage in Egypt, God makes a plan to once again dwell among humanity.

While this wasn't a total restoration of the Garden of Eden, it was an opportunity for God to once again come near His people.

The plan consisted of a tent at the center of the Israelite camp called the tabernacle where God would dwell. In the courtyard around this tent, offerings and sacrifices would be made on behalf of the sins of the people, and once a year, something special would take place.

The high priest, who was man from the tribe of Levi and one of the descendants of Aaron, would come before the Lord and actually get to enter the real, raw presence of Almighty God.

Included in the instructions given to Moses were commands for specific clothes to be made for the high priest to be worn when he entered God's presence.

The clothing was full of precious metals, gems, and vibrant colors. On the priest's forehead where all could see, a gold medallion was worn with this bold inscription: *Holy unto the Lord.*

In 1 Peter, the Apostle Peter presents to the church an incredible, revolutionary truth. He says that no longer is the priesthood limited to only a select group of people within the family of Israel. Instead, now all who put their faith in

HOLY UNTO THE LORD

Jesus—who is the *Great* High Priest and who offered Himself as the ultimate atoning sacrifice for sin—are now priests.

The Great High Priest, the only one who has ever truly lived a life that is completely "holy unto the Lord," has now made *us* priests. Something that was formerly a calling for only an elite few is now a part of the identity and calling of all believers. "You have made them to be a kingdom and priests to serve our God, and they will reign on the earth" (Revelation 5:10).

This call to be holy unto the Lord has been inscribed on our hearts as followers of Jesus. We get to set our lives apart in order to minister to God. It's now part of our calling and identity. As the Apostle Peter states: "So you must live as God's obedient children. Don't slip back into your old ways of living to satisfy your own desires. You didn't know any better then. But now you must be holy in everything you do, just as God who chose you is holy. For the Scriptures say, 'You must be holy because I am holy'" (I Peter 4:1-6).

Often people's fear regarding living a life of holiness is that it will lead to dry, lifeless legalism or that it will make them like the Pharisees, which is something we definitely need to steer clear of. We'll discuss this more in just a moment because these misconceptions allow Satan to twist the truth.

Having a true passion for holy living is not the result of legalism; rather, it is the result of love for Jesus.

What about the Pharisees?

The argument I often hear from Christians against calling the people of God to radical holiness usually begins by pointing out the legalism of the Pharisees, who were radical rule followers. The argument usually starts like this: "Jesus is the only one who could live a sinless, perfectly holy life. We could never be holy. As the Bible says, 'For everyone has sinned; we fall short of God's glorious standard' (Romans 3:23). This is why we needed Jesus to die for us."

I agree 100%.

The argument continues: "All Christians still sin occasionally. We're all just broken and hurting people. Our salvation isn't the result of our personal holiness and works; it's the result of Jesus' holiness and work on the Cross. Are you saying you won't ever sin again now that you're saved?"

Again, I would agree. It's true that we'll never be fully sinless until the day Jesus returns and eradicates unrighteousness from the earth once and for all. But here's where the argument gets into dangerous territory.

I often hear things like this: "Striving for holiness is what the Pharisees did. And Jesus rebuked them more harshly than anyone else. The Pharisees were so focused on the rules that they completely missed out on the actual relationship with God. The gospel isn't about rules; it's about relationship."

Is it true that the gospel is about God bringing humankind back into a relationship with Himself? Absolutely. But just like a covenantal marriage relationship isn't devoid of rules (like being faithful to each other as long as you live), our covenantal relationship with God is not devoid of commands and rules.

You can tell the difference between when a person is highlighting Jesus' work on the cross out of gratitude for salvation *from* their sin and when someone is highlighting Jesus' work on the cross as an excuse to *continue in* their sin. There's a difference. One is biblical. One isn't.

In Matthew 28, these are Jesus' last words to His disciples: "Therefore, go and make disciples of all the nations, baptizing them in the name of the Father and the Son and the Holy Spirit. *Teach these new disciples to obey all the commands I have given you.* And be sure of this: I am with you always, even to the end of the age" (Matthew 28:19-20, emphasis added).

As His disciples, Jesus has given us commands to obey. And those commands are for our good and for His glory.

Love for Jesus

In John 14, Jesus makes an important statement. He says, "Those who accept my commandments and obey them are the ones who love me. And because they love me, my Father will love them. And I will love them and reveal myself to each of them" (John 14:21).

HOLY UNTO THE LORD

The people Jesus promises to reveal Himself to are the people who diligently seek to keep His commands. And there's no greater joy than experiencing the nearness of God's presence in relationship with Him.

John 10:10 says that Jesus came to give us a "rich and satisfying life." All of God's commandments lead to life, not lifelessness. Walking in holiness is one of the greatest keys to experiencing the fullness of joy that the Father desires for us to walk in as His children.

Hebrews 12:14 says, "Work at living in peace with everyone, and work at living a holy life (some translations say *pursue holiness*), for those who are not holy will not see the Lord."

Here, stated simply, is the difference between a pure pursuit of holiness and a legalistic one: A pure pursuit of holiness comes from a burning desire to see and exalt God. A legalistic pursuit of holiness comes from a desire for other people to see and exalt us.

Our motivation matters.

This is why Jesus rebuked the Pharisees. It wasn't because of their desire for holiness but because of their desire for people to idolize them as being more righteous and holy than other people.

A Pharisee obeys to exalt himself. A disciple obeys to exalt and love Jesus.

HOLY UNTO THE LORD

As 1 Peter says, "But now you must be holy in everything you do, just as God who chose you is holy" (1 Peter 1:15). The truth is not, *because Jesus is holy, we don't have to be holy.* But rather, *because Jesus is holy, we are empowered to live holy, too.*

4

COSTLY WORSHIP

I will not present burnt offerings to the LORD my God that have cost me nothing.

2 SAMUEL 24:24

Take a moment to ask yourself: Why do I worship?

In the 21st century American church, the majority of us know little about sacrificial worship. When we come together as the church or come before the Lord in times of private devotions, the primary mindset we often have is to *get* something from God rather than to *give* something to God.

Think about it. We come to the Lord in worship, hoping that it will act as our weekly pick-me-up, hoping that as we sing songs at church it will quiet our anxieties and lift our burdens. We read the Word with a quiet demand for some new revelation or for God to speak to us.

Now, the desires for God to speak to us, lift our burdens, and quiet our anxieties are not wrong by any means. These are parts of who God is! He's our healer, our comforter, and our loving Father. But the question to ask is this: Am I worshiping God to *get* something from Him or to *give* something to Him?

If we're worshiping God to only get instead of to give, we have subtly made ourselves the object of our worship.

In Matthew 6, Jesus gives us a beautiful glimpse into the Father's heart for us. He says,

> *That is why I tell you not to worry about everyday life—whether you have enough food and drink, or enough clothes to wear. Isn't life more than food, and your body more than clothing? Look at the birds. They don't plant or harvest or store food in barns, for your heavenly Father feeds them. And aren't you far more valuable to him than they are?*

MATTHEW 6:25-26

Jesus continues by saying, "So don't worry about these things, saying, 'What will we eat? What will we drink? What will we wear?' These things dominate the thoughts of unbelievers, but your heavenly Father already knows all your needs" (Matthew 6:31-32).

And then He makes a statement that has profound implications for our lives. Jesus states, "Seek the Kingdom of God above all else, and live righteously, and he will give you everything you need" (Matthew 6:33).

We have a good heavenly Father who knows all of our needs before we tell Him about them. He knows our hurts, stresses, and pains. He knows our shortcomings and weaknesses. And it is with that knowledge that He tells us not to worry about our everyday needs, but instead to seek His kingdom.

Isn't it true that we often spend the most time thinking and praying about the very things Jesus told us not to worry about at all? But armed with the knowledge that God will provide all of our needs, we can come before Him solely to pour out our praise and worship. To give Him our very lives.

And when we do, we'll find that we receive more than we could ever have imagined.

A Living Sacrifice

The people of the Bible knew nothing of empty-handed worship. One read through the book of Leviticus makes it clear that no one came to the tabernacle or the temple without something to give to God.

We know that Jesus' final and ultimate sacrifice on the cross has done away with the Old Covenant that included sacrificing animals to cover our sins. So as New Covenant believers, what do we offer to God? Paul answers this for us: "Therefore, I urge you, brothers and sisters, in view of God's mercy, to offer your bodies as a living sacrifice, holy and pleasing to God—this is your true and proper worship" (Romans 12:1 NIV).

COSTLY WORSHIP

When we come before the Lord, we are no longer coming with a sacrifice of lambs and goats, but to offer our very lives to Him. And, just to be clear, we're not offering our bodies to God as if He is requesting some kind of human sacrifice. Remember what Romans 12:2 says from Chapter 1? "Don't copy the behavior and customs of this world, but let God transform you into a new person by changing the way you think. Then you will learn to know God's will for you, which is good and pleasing and perfect." We offer our lives to God as living sacrifices by not copying the ways of the culture around us and by conforming our lives to God's Word in loving obedience.

I have often caught myself in the mindset of coming to the Lord in worship with the sole goal of receiving, not coming to offer something to Him.

Something that helps me posture my heart is to picture myself like an Israelite bringing my lamb to the temple to sacrifice before the Lord.

I do this in prayer, when reading the Word, or in gatherings with other believers. And I ask myself, "What can I bring to the Lord today? What is my sacrifice of praise?"

Is it a greater level of surrender? Is it a deeper level of grief and repentance for my sin? Is it a greater level of action and obedience to Jesus' commands? Whatever it is, I want to offer something to Jesus today. I don't want to offer empty, cheap sacrifices of praise but, rather, something that actually costs me something.

True Worship

Here's the reality: True worship will cost us something.

King David understood this. In 2 Samuel 24, David is preparing to bring an offering to the Lord. So he comes to a man and offers to buy his property and animals in order to make a sacrifice to God. The man is so honored that the king would come to his home that he offers to simply give the land and animals to David for free.

If anyone in the Bible understood the heart of true worship, it was David. And it's here that we get a glimpse into David's understanding of worship. He replies to the man, "No, I insist on buying it, for I will not present burnt offerings to the Lord my God that have cost me nothing" (2 Samuel 24:24).

I will not offer to God that which costs me nothing. This is the heart of true worship.

Our Gift to God

Imagine there's a man who wants to marry the love of his life. He's found the woman he wants to be committed to above all others. When he goes out to buy her an engagement ring, he's not going to go to Dollar General. He's going to go to the finest jeweler he can afford.

If he has to work extra hours to afford it, he will. If he has to choose not to buy something that he personally wants in order to be able to get the ring for her, he will. Why? Because

COSTLY WORSHIP

he wants to give her something that shows her how much she's worth to him. This is what costly worship communicates to God.

True love gives. "For God so loved the world that He *gave his only Son…*" (John 3:16 NIV, emphasis added). A love for God that only takes and never gives is not true love.

This type of worshiper comes before God daily in gratitude for His mercy through Jesus on the Cross, saying, "Lord Jesus, here's my life. Whatever you ask me to do, wherever you call me to go, my life is yours– whatever it costs me. If it costs me my comfort, here's my life. If it costs me popularity or causes me to be ridiculed, here's my life. If it costs me worldly pleasure (which it certainly will), here's my life. Even if it costs me life itself, I give myself completely to you."

Worship that costs us nothing communicates a low value for who God is and what He's done for us.

Now, I want to be careful here because it may sound like I'm proposing going out and finding hard things to do for God simply because they're hard. That would be legalism, and it's not what the Lord invites us into. What I am saying is that, as the people of God, we should follow His example of love with a willingness to give Him everything, no matter the cost.

To those who would say that this still sounds like legalism, Jesus tells His followers in Mark 8:35, "For whoever wants to save his life will lose it, but whoever loses his life for me will find it" (NIV).

It's through first surrendering our lives completely to God that we are positioned to receive all that He has for us.

It's when we completely surrender our lives to Jesus as living sacrifices that we find true life in Him. A living sacrifice is completely surrendered to the Holy Spirit of Jesus. Whatever He asks us to do, wherever He asks us to go, we say yes out of a burning love for Jesus.

The world tells us we'll find life by *getting* what we want. Jesus says we'll find life by *giving* Him everything.

5

WHERE IS THE POWER OF GOD?

If my people, who are called by my name, will humble themselves and pray and seek my face and turn from their wicked ways, then I will hear from heaven, and I will forgive their sin and will heal their land.

2 CHRONICLES 7:14

It's easy to look at the church of the New Testament versus the church in America today and ask the question: Where is the power of God?

In the early church, God was moving in powerful signs and wonders. The miraculous was a constant reality.

A.W. Tozer is attributed to have said, "If the Holy Spirit was withdrawn from the church today, 95 percent of what we do would go on and no one would know the difference. If the Holy Spirit had been withdrawn from the New Testament church, 95 percent of what they did would stop, and everybody would know the difference."

So again we ask, "What happened to the power of God? Where did it go?" While this is an important question, I believe the lack of power in the church is a fruit of the problem, not the root of the problem.

Instead of asking where His power went, we should be asking, "What happened to the purity of the people of God?"

God Is Still Holy

In the first chapter of this book, we discussed the holiness of God. At times, our actions unveil a (faulty) belief in our hearts that the God of the Old Testament was holier than the God of the New Testament.

We act like the God of the Old Testament was righteous, incredibly holy, and even dangerous to draw near. He was extremely powerful, perfectly pure, and breathtakingly awesome.

But we act like the God of the New Testament is solely a gentle, loving, compassionate Father who is holy but doesn't require our reverence or fear anymore because of what Jesus did on the cross.

But Jesus didn't come to give us a *different* understanding of God. Rather, He came to give us a *fuller* understanding of God.

He didn't replace a holy God with a loving Father. Instead, He revealed that our holy God is *also* a loving Father.

WHERE IS THE POWER OF GOD?

Today, we often behave as if we believe that because Jesus paid the penalty for our sins, we no longer need to have awe and reverence when drawing near to God. Many act as if we no longer need to be concerned with our personal holiness and conduct when we approach Him.

We justify our lack of reverence by saying, "Jesus loves us just the way we are. Jesus wants me to come as I am. Therefore, I can draw near to God without worrying about His holiness–or my own."

But let's take a look at a New Testament example that should cause us to rethink how we approach God.

Ananias and Sapphira

In the book of Acts, the church is in true revival. The power of God is on constant display. Miracles are taking place left and right. And the masses are repenting from sin and turning to faith in Jesus. God was truly in their midst.

I want to make a quick theological distinction here. You might be thinking, "Isn't God always in our midst?" In a sense, this is true. One of the key truths about God is that He's omnipresent, which means He's everywhere at all times. God doesn't have to travel to go from one place to another. He's everywhere at once. As Solomon said, "The heavens, even the highest heavens, cannot contain Him" (2 Chronicles 2:6 ESV).

HOLY UNTO THE LORD

But there's a difference between God's omnipresence and His *manifest* presence. While God is everywhere at once, at times He chooses to manifest Himself in a way that is beyond the baseline of His omnipresence. Several examples of this are when the Holy Spirit was poured out on the day of Pentecost, when people were healed, or when the cloud of glory filled the temple.

And if the people of God desire to live in the manifest presence of God, there's a different level of accountability and reverence that's required. This is what was happening in the book of Acts. His manifest presence was being made known among His people.

It's in this context that Acts 5 tells the story of Ananias and Sapphira. At this time, all of the believers were being moved by the Holy Spirit to sell all of their possessions and bring the profits to the apostles so that they could distribute the money to make sure everyone in the church's needs were met. This in itself was a miracle.

And during this time, a couple named Ananias and Sapphira sold all of their possessions as well. But instead of bringing all of the profits to the apostles, they kept some for themselves. This might not have been a big deal, except that when they brought the money to the apostles, they claimed that they hadn't kept any for themselves, which was a lie.

In the words of my friend Danny Rangel, "They wanted the status without the sacrifice."

WHERE IS THE POWER OF GOD?

When this happened, in that atmosphere of God's manifest presence, they both immediately dropped dead (Acts 5:5-10).

The Word says that when this happened, "great fear gripped the entire church and everyone else who heard what had happened" (Acts 5:11).

Notice that it doesn't simply say that fear gripped those outside the church but that it gripped the entire New Testament church with a fresh and holy fear of the Lord.

Now, this passage shouldn't cause us to fear that we're suddenly going to get struck by a lightning bolt the next time we sin. What it *should* cause us to do is soberly reconsider the seriousness of our sin in the light of a holy God who desires to dwell among us.

It's common today to hear people pray–as I have prayed many times myself–"Oh God, would you pour out your Spirit on your people!" While this is absolutely a prayer we should be praying, I think we should pray it with great reverence in our hearts. We should pray it with a healthy fear of what it might actually mean for a holy God to be in our midst. It's not something to be taken lightly.

If *My* People

In 2 Chronicles, God makes a promise that has been echoed by the people of God for generations. I've heard it quoted countless times by those who are praying for revival, but I believe its message is often misused and misinterpreted.

Second Chronicles 7:14 says, "If my people, who are called by my name, will humble themselves and pray and seek my face and turn from their wicked ways, then I will hear from heaven, and I will forgive their sin and will heal their land."

This is the way this verse is often quoted when people pray for God to move in America: "Oh God, would you cause our nation to repent! Cause our politicians to repent! Cause our president to repent! Cause the people in the abortion clinics to repent! Cause Hollywood to repent! Come and heal our land!"

But this is not at all what the verse says. God actually says, "If *my people*... will turn from their wicked ways... then I will hear, forgive, and revive them." It's not a call for the people outside the church to repent; it's a call for the people of God themselves to repent and turn from their wickedness.

"Well," you might think, "I don't know that I have any *wicked* ways to repent of..."

God's Word has a response for this: "If we claim we have no sin, we are only fooling ourselves and not living in the truth... If we claim we have not sinned, we are calling God a liar and showing that his Word has no place in our hearts" (1 John 1:8, 10).

But here's the good news. His Word also says, "But if we confess our sins to him, he is faithful and just to forgive us our sins and to cleanse us from all wickedness" (1 John 1:9).

So What Does This Mean for Us?

The Bible says that "Jesus Christ is the same yesterday, today, and forever" (Hebrews 13:8). This means He has not changed. He's the same God now as He was back then. Just as holy. Just as awesome. Just as demanding of our awe and reverence.

So what does that mean for us? It means that if we truly want to see the power of God restored to the church in our day, we should also have a fierce desire to see the purity of the people of God restored in our day–starting in our own lives.

6

IN THE WORLD BUT NOT OF IT

I have given them your word. And the world hates them because they do not belong to the world, just as I do not belong to the world. I'm not asking you to take them out of the world, but to keep them safe from the evil one. They do not belong to this world any more than I do. Make them holy by your truth; teach them your word, which is truth.

JOHN 17:14-17

As believers in Jesus, we aren't called to leave civilization and go build a monastery up on a mountain so that we don't have to interact with unbelievers (as some have done).

We're called to be the light of the world (Matthew 5:14) and witnesses (Acts 1:8) to the truth and power of the gospel. This requires that we be in the world.

However, as believers, we're called to be set apart. To be holy as He is holy. To be *in* the world, but not *of* the world.

A Common Fear

Recently, as I've preached about the church being called to holiness and consecration (which means to be set apart *from* the world and set apart *for* Jesus), I've been approached by people that have apprehensions.

"The concept of consecration scares me," they'll say. Often, they explain that this fear flows from a picture of themselves stuck in a lifeless religion, which, as we discussed earlier, is a lie from the enemy.

Another reason people are hesitant comes from a belief (whether they were intentionally taught this or not) that the only way to be set apart for God is to become a pastor.

Maybe you've felt this way before. Perhaps you've felt like God has gifted you and called you to a certain occupation, but if you truly wanted to serve God, it meant laying it down to go into full-time ministry. This simply isn't biblical.

Only a portion of the body of Christ will be called by God to be pastors, missionaries, and worship leaders. Many will be called to be businessmen and businesswomen, entrepreneurs, musicians, artists, teachers, politicians, and so on. I would dare to say that occupations in the secular sphere don't require less consecration but actually require an even more intense level of consecration to God in some respects.

Biblical Examples

Some great examples of those who weren't called into traditional ministry roles but were used by God to impact a generation are Bezalel, Daniel, Joseph, Nehemiah, Esther, Shadrach, Meshach, Abed-Nego, Lydia, and Cornelius.

Bezalel was an artisan. Joseph was a government official, as were Daniel, Shadrach, Meshach, Abed-Nego, and Nehemiah. Esther was a queen. Lydia was a businesswoman. Cornelius was a Roman soldier. And these are just a few examples!

Perhaps the best example of what it looks like to be in the world but not of the world is Daniel. So let's take a closer look at his life.

Holiness in the Secular World

Many people use Daniel as an example of how one can be called to a "secular" industry. But Daniel's life probably looks a lot different than most modern-day believers'.

Outside of Jesus, who was sinless, a case could be made for Daniel being one of the most righteous men who ever lived. And Daniel wasn't a priest or a Levite or a pastor! He was one of the highest-ranking officials in the most powerful, sin-soaked nation on earth: Babylon.

When Daniel first arrives in Babylon, the king offers him the most delicious food and drink in the entire kingdom. But rather than defile himself (because this meat had been

IN THE WORLD BUT NOT OF IT

used as sacrifices to false gods), he chooses instead to only eat vegetables and drink water rather than break God's covenant commands (Daniel 1:12).

I don't know about you, but I love meat. And choosing to only eat vegetables and drink water rather than eat meat would grow pretty old pretty fast…but not for Daniel.

Daniel goes on to experience such incredible promotion from God that it makes him an enemy in the sight of the other Babylonian officials, so much so that they trick the king into making a law that says no one is allowed to pray to anyone or anything other than the king for thirty days.

Why trick him into making this law? They do it because they know Daniel prays to God three times a day… *every* day! And this isn't just a give-thanks-before-you-eat kind of prayer. Daniel is kneeling before God, fervently praising and giving thanks, repenting of sin, asking God to search his heart, and repenting for the sins of his people. Three times a day he is crying out for God to deliver his people from exile and to restore Jerusalem.

Even when he learns of the law that makes his daily prayer routine illegal, he is not deterred. Daniel 6:10 says, "But when Daniel learned that the law had been signed, he went home and knelt down as usual in his upstairs room, with his windows open toward Jerusalem. He prayed three times a day, just as he had always done, giving thanks to his God."

Daniel's refusal to compromise gets him a death sentence of being fed alive to lions. But God miraculously delivers him, and the ones who tried to kill him are thrown to the lions instead.

This is the type of consecration it takes to be truly in the world but not of it. Daniel was tenaciously devoted to God.

Friends with the World. Enemies of God.

But here's where the lines often get blurred. Many people I've encountered who say they feel called to a certain field, whether it be arts and entertainment, business, politics, etc., are using the term "calling" simply to mask a lust to fulfill the American Dream. They want to be popular in today's culture. They want the acclaim, the applause, and the accolades of the world.

Many of us truly will be called to have occupations that are outside of traditional ministry roles, but there's something very wrong when our "calling" only makes us popular with the world and never causes us to be persecuted by the world.

The Apostle Paul says to his spiritual son Timothy in his final letter before he was executed, "Yes, and *everyone* who wants to live a godly life in Christ Jesus will suffer persecution" (2 Timothy 3:12, emphasis added).

If what we claim is our calling only gives us worldly prestige, then I would venture to say it's not a calling from God but rather a dream of our own hearts and, ultimately, an idol that we're worshiping.

You may say, "Who are you to judge someone's motives?" But here's what the Bible says: "You can identify them by their fruit, that is, by the way they act." (Matthew 7:16).

The fruit of their lives reveals their hearts' motives. They usually haven't led anyone to Christ or made any disciples in their field. Instead, they end up looking more and more like the world the longer they're there.

Too often, those who say they feel called to "impact the industry" end up with the industry impacting them. In order to be accepted, they start to look more like their non-believing coworkers, rather than impacting their coworkers to look more like Jesus.

Then there are others who genuinely go into industries with good intentions but often begin to forget the words of Psalm 75:6-7: "Exaltation comes neither from the east nor from the west nor from the south. But God is the judge: He puts down one and exalts another" (NKJV).

They begin to seek the favor of man over the favor of God. The favor of God doesn't always–or even often–make you popular with the world. But it will make you effective in the world.

Seeking favor from the world will cause you to compromise. Seeking favor from God will cause you to have convictions.

A Friend of Sinners?

You might be wondering, "But wasn't Jesus a friend of sinners? Aren't we called to be friends of sinners too?"

The answer is, "*Absolutely*!" But there's a difference between being a friend of sinners and a friend of the world.

A friend of the world is someone who gets "cozy" with sin. They get comfortable with the ways and values of the world instead of staying committed to the ways and values of the Word.

James 4:4 says, "You adulterers! Don't you realize that friendship with the world makes you an enemy of God? I say it again: If you want to be a friend of the world, you make yourself an enemy of God."

John 17:14 says, "And the world hates them because they do not belong to the world, just as I do not belong to the world."

On the other hand, a friend of sinners is someone who loves and listens to those who don't know Jesus. They love them as they are and then share the life-transforming truth and power of the gospel with them.

You'll notice that while Jesus would often hang around sinners, He never started looking more like them. Instead, the sinners who followed Jesus started looking more like Him.

IN THE WORLD BUT NOT OF IT

A friend of the world ends up becoming like the world. A friend of sinners helps sinners find Jesus so they can become more like Him.

A Modern-Day Example

A few months ago I was having coffee with a pastor who told me a story about a man who worked in corporate America for many years. This man was a fervent follower of Jesus and was constantly sharing his faith with his coworkers and fellow executives. As you might guess, this didn't make everyone at the company extremely happy.

But there was a problem. This man did such an incredible job and was so diligent, responsible, and excellent at his work that they couldn't fire him. And for as long as he was at the company, every single year they both threatened to fire him if he kept sharing his faith, and they also promoted him! This is what it looks like to be a follower of Jesus who's called to be in the world but not of it.

As followers of Jesus, we're called to trust that God is the one who promotes and exalts. Our job is to be set apart from the world and consecrated to Him; to be faithful to His commands and His calling, no matter what we look like to the world.

7

A CONSECRATED GENERATION

Joshua told the people, "Consecrate yourselves, for tomorrow the LORD will do amazing things among you."

JOSHUA 3:5 ESV

What is consecration? It's not a term that we use much in the 21st century, but it's a biblical concept of great importance and promise.

I think the simplest and best definition of consecration that I've heard comes from John Mark Comer who says, "Consecration is the giving up of things that other people consider to be normal in order to more fully give yourself over to God."[4]

A few prime examples of consecration in the Bible are the prophet Samuel, John the Baptist, the prophet Elijah, and the Apostle Paul.

One thing to notice from this list is that each of these men lived in unusual days and were used by God in unusual ways.

A CONSECRATED GENERATION

Samuel lived in a time of immense corruption among the priesthood when there was no prophet in the land to help the people hear from and follow God.

Elijah was used to bring down one of the most evil and corrupt monarchies in Israel's history.

John the Baptist was the prophetic voice that called the people of God to repentance in order to prepare the way for the arrival of Jesus the Messiah.

In times of great darkness and great corruption, people of great consecration are needed.

The Apostle Paul stepped into Corinth, which was one of the most sexually immoral, demonically influenced, and corrupt cities in the ancient world (imagine Las Vegas on steroids) and saw it turned upside down as he called the people to repentance and holiness.

Paul was writing to the Corinthians, reminding them of how they had been washed from a life of sin, when he said, "Everything is permissible, but not everything is beneficial" (1 Corinthians 6:12 BSB). In other words, when we give our lives to Christ we stop asking the question, *What can I get away with without it being a sin?* And instead we start asking, *What things are going to feed my love and commitment to Jesus the most?*

Someone who's consecrated isn't looking to see how close to the line they can get without sinning. They're looking to see how close to God they can get without reservation.

We live in a day when corruption in the church has been a recurring headline. We see leader after leader falling into sin or walking away altogether, and a lust for money and fame in church leadership. And in a day when corruption is the headline, we need a great revival of consecration.

The World Is Yet to See

D. L. Moody was one of the 19th century's greatest evangelists. It's said that he traveled over a million miles (before the days of airplanes), spoke to more than a hundred million people (before the days of television), and most likely led nearly a million people to Christ.

One day, when he was spending time with a friend of his named Henry Varley, Henry said something that would grip the heart of D. L. Moody for decades to come.

He said, "The world has yet to see what God will do with a man fully consecrated to him."

Moody would repeat these words many times throughout his life; they were like a fire in his bones. He would go on to say, "With God's help, I aim to be that man."

Undoubtedly, D. L. Moody's consecration to God played a key part in how mightily God used him.

The Eyes of the Lord Are Searching

Anyone who's known me for any length of time knows that possibly my favorite verse in the entire Bible is 2 Chronicles

A CONSECRATED GENERATION

16:9. I have this verse printed on a banner that hangs over my desk.

If you're not familiar with this verse, let me first give us some context for what's happening in this part of scripture. At this moment in history, the city of Jerusalem is under siege by an enemy who's much larger and more powerful than they are. Every time they look over the walls of the city, they see an army too great to count camping in the distance.

The danger they're facing is not simply being conquered but being completely starved to death and slaughtered, even their wives and children. And in this time of great pressure and uncertainty, Asa, the king of Judah, has a crisis of faith.

Instead of turning to God for help, he goes to the nearby nations who don't believe in God and pays them as mercenaries to come and help fight against their enemy. And this plan works…or so it seems.

When the dust settles and Jerusalem appears to be out of danger, a prophet comes to King Asa and brings him a message from God.

Essentially his message is this: "You have made a foolish mistake. Don't you remember all of the times God has delivered you in the past? Why didn't you trust that He would do it again? And now, because you trusted in the kings of other nations instead of God, the even greater victory that God wanted to bring you has slipped from your

HOLY UNTO THE LORD

hands. Because of this, you will continually be at war with the nations around you."

And then the prophet makes this statement: "For the eyes of the LORD search the whole earth in order to strengthen those whose hearts are fully committed to him" (2 Chronicles 16:9).

What an incredible reality! One translation says, "...to show Himself strong on behalf of those whose hearts are fully devoted to Him."

The eyes of God are searching. He's not sitting back passively on His throne thinking, "Maybe I'll show myself strong on behalf of my people, maybe I won't." No, He's actively looking to show Himself strong in power *for* and *through* His people.

It's clear that He's looking for one simple thing. He's not looking for talent, good looks, economic status, popularity, or anything of that sort. The Bible says He's looking for fully devoted hearts.

And a fully devoted heart will be evidenced by a fully devoted life. A consecrated life.

You might be popular or you might not. You might be blessed with a multitude of talents, or, like me, you might not. You might be considered good-looking by a lot of people, have a lot of money, and have a high social status, or you might not. But the good news is that God is looking for the one thing that everyone can give Him: a fully devoted heart and life. A consecrated life.

The Purposes of God for Our Generation

A few days ago I was listening to the book of Acts on audio, and a verse I'd read many times before caught my attention in a new way.

Acts 13:36 says, "For David, after he had served the purpose of God in his own generation, fell asleep" (ESV).

When I heard that I thought, "That's what I want to be said of my life when I die, that when I pass away, it would be said that I fulfilled the purpose of God for my life in my generation."

And although I believe this verse can be in reference to the fact that in God's perfect sovereignty every human being fulfills His purposes in one way or another, I want my life to be spent ardently serving God and His mission.

Consecrated men and women are ones who give their whole life, every part of it, with every breath in their lungs, to know God and serve the purposes of God in their generation.

When I'm on my deathbed, looking back over my life, I want it to be true that I held nothing back from God. That I left it all on the field. That I gave Him everything. Don't you?

HOLY UNTO THE LORD

Let's be that generation. A consecrated, whole-hearted, fully devoted generation. Holy unto the Lord.

REFERENCES

1. Owen, John. 1656. *Mortification of Sin.*
2. Spurgeon, Charles H. 1869. "A Well-ordered Life." *Spurgeon's Sermons*, (June).
3. Lewis, C.S. 1950. *The Lion, The Witch, and The Wardrobe.* New York, New York: Macmillan.
4. Comer, John Mark. n.d. "Preaching." The Art of Teaching. https://artofteaching.mykajabi.com/products/the-art-of-teaching-masterclass/categories/2149449199/posts/2154509335

Made in the USA
Coppell, TX
03 October 2022